*By the same author:*

My Life
with a Brahmin Family
*1972*

To Live Within
*1971*

The Dedicated:
A Biography of Nivedita
*1953*

Shakti

A Far West Press Book

# SHAKTI

A Spiritual Experience

by Lizelle Reymond

Introduction by Shri Anirvan

Alfred A. Knopf, New York, 1974

This is a Borzoi Book published by Alfred A. Knopf, Inc.
English translation Copyright © 1974 by Lizelle Reymond.
All rights reserved under International
and Pan-American Copyright Conventions.
Published in the United States by Alfred A. Knopf, Inc.,
New York, and simultaneously in Canada by Random House
of Canada Limited, Toronto.
Distributed by Random House, Inc., New York.
Originally published in France by Derain
under the title *Shakti ou l'Expérience Spirituelle*, 1951.
Copyright 1951 by Lizelle Reymond.

Library of Congress Cataloging in Publication Data:
Reymond, Lizelle, date. Shakti.
1. Shaktism. I. Title.
BL1245.S4R43   1974      294.5'42      74-7725
ISBN 0-394-49339-7

Manufactured in the United States of America
First Edition

# Introduction

The author has prepared these four essays in the Hindu manner, plunging into the direct experience in order to give us something we are able to touch from the Divine Shakti. Doubtless the Western reader will be somewhat surprised at the absence of logic and all dogmas in this presentation. But this will not trouble the Hindu reader. "We feel this is true," he thinks, and therefore no explanation is necessary. We describe our experiences logically only when we must attain a precise and definite aim. Otherwise life flows unchecked, always new. And this life in freedom is Shakti.

It is strange to note that in the vast literature on Shakti, although numerous texts exist with the aim of "indicating the methods for attaining Shakti," there is not a single work analyzing what Shakti is. The treatises are the *Paddhati Granthas*, which describe in detail all the rituals to be known.

The reason for this is that Shakti is inexplicable. Whoever wishes to study a philosophy of Shakti must create it totally for his personal use, for his own satisfaction, because no trace of it exists in the tradition. Shaktism is the ensemble of spiritual experience lived with a background of Shivaic philosophy. In no instance can one expect to find the theory of Shakti clearly set forth.

Thus no verbal teaching exists. The following dialogue between Khepa Baba, a nineteenth-century tantric master of Bengal, and his disciple is cited.

DISCIPLE: "Tell me what is Tara."*
MASTER: "Tara is the Void."
DISCIPLE: "Tell me something more about it."
MASTER: "Be quiet. Not another word. Do what I
     tell you to do."

To explain Shakti without the experience of it is like speaking of an electric shock where there is no electricity. Shakti becomes manifest at the very moment when the psychic being reacts violently to being possessed by it. It is a forceful descent of power, a transference from guru to disciple, and not necessarily according to one of the many traditional methods.

Silence plays an important role in this transmission. All the great masters agree on this point. The Advaitists often speak of the beneficent expression of the guru immersed in absolute silence. Only his subtle

* The symbolism of the Divine Mother, who saves the world.

smile, evoking a radiation of joy, is the sign of his power. The disciple must know the same silence in complete passivity. He who gives and he who receives are thus the two poles in the Void, in which the potential power vibrates.

The *Katha Upanishad* reveals to us that the giver of power is Yama—Death itself—to Nachiketas, the young boy who personifies the eternal youth aspiring to know—who does not yet know but who is going to know.

*Marvelous the one who reveals the power*
*and resplendent the one who receives it.*
*Marvelous is the one who listens*
*and resplendent is the one who teaches.*

According to tradition in the *Puranas*,* these two personages are represented by Shiva and his wife, Parvati; in Samkhya philosophy by the Absolute (Purusha) and the manifestation of primordial nature (Prakriti).

The transmission of power between guru and dis-

---

*Sacred Sanskrit writings concerning divine revelation and creation, supposed to have been compiled by the poet Vyasa and written between the fourth century B.C. and the fourteenth A.D.

ciple in absolute silence is a return to initial primitivism, where the concept of the transubstantiation of one element into another is a natural fact. This is what takes place in the psychic being and what is pointed out in the *Brihadaranyaka Upanishad*. After the absorption of all knowledge, the psychic being must try to rediscover the naïveté of a child. The crowning achievement of spiritual life is the look of wonder in the "child" who sees the vast universe for the first time, and is not offended by anything because everything is integrated in the Mother. This means to restore individual consciousness to its original simplicity with the whole mass of experiences in the background.

The *Chandogya Upanishad* tells us that there is only one important teaching: All experience is a derivation from original consciousness. This consciousness in its original simplicity is the "child." This child is Shakti.

Shri Anirvan

*Haimavati, India, 1972*

Part One

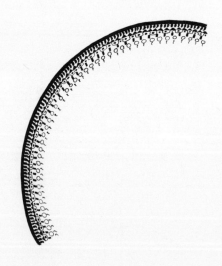

Although numerous treatises exist in Sanskrit, written throughout the ages by the great masters to explain and determine what Shakti is, none of them successfully explains its nature. But this is not all that is known. A complete oral literature of equal importance also exists, transmitted from father to son or from guru to disciple. For example, there is such a commentary of the *Chandi*,* preserved by a family of rajahs and recited in its entirety every day for generations, but which has never been written down, even on palm leaves. Shakti is a complete science. This word, "Shakti," has been translated into English in different ways. It may be divine or cosmic energy, the active and conscious force of God, the play of destruction and creation, the Divine Power. It is said to be almost synonymous with primordial nature, "that which makes the impossible possible" and "that which is beyond Maya while still being Maya."† The *Shvetashvatara Upanishad* says, "Know that Maya is Prakriti, and that the Great Lord rules Maya."

*A part of the *Markandaya Purana*, celebrating the victories of the Divine Mother.
†Shankaracharya. Here Maya is given as illusion.

# 4

I shall try to relate as simply as possible, in a real and practical way, some of the concepts of which I gradually became aware in India that bear directly on Shakti. This empirical method is most certainly outside all logical and critical accounts of the subject, but it allows the important points to be outlined in order to penetrate to the heart of Hinduism.

Shakti can be an aim in itself, as well as a means. At the same time and in both cases, it is the omnipotent and indeterminate force of which everyone in India is more or less aware, without always wishing to admit it for fear of being judged superstitious. I must admit that all the aspects of Shakti, whatever they may be, are complementary to each other and have come at the right time to help me to take a step forward. I have only to be engaged in living—without attachment to any one of these aspects—in a rhythm where I feel the deep harmony of this eternal force operating around me and in me.

Shakti is not definable by the words "concrete" or "abstract." It is at once everything and nothing, fullness and emptiness, and at the same time it is behind these opposites. In order to speak of it, there is practically no other method possible than to call on personal experience—which, moreover, is not any more subjective than the opinion each one of us forms about Truth. Between the one who speaks and the one who listens, the very vibration in which the idea lives is Shakti in all its power, passing from the vessel that contains to the vessel that receives—and these two vessels are also Shakti in its power.

Is Shakti a sensation? I have often asked myself this. It appears so before coming into the fullness of its force. It is only perceptible in relation to a more or less refined level of consciousness on the part of the one who is seeking it, and is ready to receive it in his innermost being. Felt and assimilated, it immediately loses all the qualities by which it was recognized on the mental level. Hence, the difficulty in speaking of it. It is somewhat like having a desire for milk and then describing it in a thousand ways to a blind man who delights in milk but has never seen it!

In spiritual evolution Shakti is "cause" and "effect," and at the same time their support: the concept that we call "time" is a necessary security to support our logical reasoning. Of the three, "time" is the least necessary element, rather artificial, because it is essentially mental. When Shakti is contented and merciful, according to the *Chandi*, it is the cause that liberates us from the cycle of births and deaths; when it does not grant its grace, it is the cause of all our slavery.

In India, Shakti is not an abstraction. It is a part of daily life. There is not a thought, a gesture, or an action which does not contain it, whereas in Europe this concept is nonexistent and has produced, consequently, the divorce between man and creation. If I had known about this, even only intellectually, perhaps the following would have opened my eyes. At a certain period I suffered from severe anemia, which the attending physician, after having unsuccessfully tried several remedies, decided to treat with a remedy whose function was to "stabilize the interaction of the vital elements within me." Shakti is exactly this power. It is that which links the dancer to the music. It is that which establishes a link between all things, holding them in interdependence and in relation fixed at a level that goes beyond us—the stars around their sun, in their place, and in their function as grains of sand on the beach. It is the Presence, invisible and constant, which sustains the world, linking form and name. Life is born in its vibration. God creates ceaselessly, delighting in His creation, in a harmony known to Him alone. Shakti is His power and His essence.

It also represents the feminine element, the Divine Mother, whose name comes quite naturally to the lips of those without hope. Each Hindu speaks of his Divine Mother with a surprising and disarming familiarity. Each woman, even a little girl, is also called "Mother" because, says the *Chandi*, "Thou art all women."

But Shakti is before all that exists, even before life. It is what Brahman* has not yet become. It is the Energy-Void in the living silence, where the whirlwind will be born—the whirlwind from which the sacred Sound will issue forth, the active God all-powerful and eternal Creator. The sacred Sound is the guardian of the gate of silence, the first manifestation. Here one thinks of the Gospel of St. John: "In the beginning was the Word, the Word was with God and the Word was God."†

God, nature, men, animals, plants, minerals or, bet-

---

* The Undifferentiated Absolute.
† Gospel of St. John, I:1.

ter yet, all the subtle elements and all the gross elements come from Shakti, exist through it, and contain it as a whole in each particle. Movement is Shakti, and this is so true that without it even Brahma, Vishnu, and Shiva, the three gods of the Hindu Trimurti, are without expression.* Without the Divine Shakti, Shiva would only be a body without life and the symbolism of Ma Kali† disappears. Ma Kali only exists in relation to Shiva, a dual movement in a manifest world.

If India could explain to the West, desirous of understanding the nature of Shakti in its subtle and gross elements and the force that connects them, one would have the explanation that spirit and matter are *one*. It is a fact rejected in the West at a time when India not only affirms it, but lives it. From the concept of the intimate contact between man and God Shri Ramakrishna said, "Yes, I can make you touch God as I touch Him."

The practical difficulty is that the essence of Shakti is terrifying and surpasses human understanding. The

*Shankaracharya, *Saundarya-Lahari*, trans.
S. Subrahmanya Sastri Ma, 1937.
† The Divine Mother, cosmic energy symbolizing time.

West has discovered atomic energy and has released it toward a dangerous course without taking into account that Shakti is potentially this power, for better or for worse, an active force in a free state. To capture it, to use it, is to perform black magic on a grand scale, and to risk what happens when forces are released without knowing how to neutralize them. To wish to use these forces on the physical level is to assume the role of God and to satisfy unrestrained egos, positive or negative. These forces are constantly acting by themselves on the subtle and nonphysical levels. The Hindus know these forces as well as the Westerners know their laboratory sciences. But the Hindus make little use of them because in daily life each disciple who lives in the shadow of a great guru knows that the latter has the force of Shakti at his disposal and can use it at will. The miracle is that men will always need it in order to believe, and that it is given to them when necessary. Except for a great master, who can determine the necessity of a miracle, which is nothing more than creating a Void where Shakti comes into play in full power? Shri Ramakrishna speaks of a disciple who, while meditating on a beach, was suddenly disturbed by a violent storm. "Let the wind stop," he ordered. The wind stopped immediately, but as a result a heavily loaded boat proceeding under full sail capsized and all of the passengers were drowned.

The sacred Sound that guards the silence of Shakti plays the role of bringing Shakti forth, whenever invoked, to manifest itself. It is a resonant syllable called a bija-mantra, which whenever spoken establishes contact with the divine vibration. The best known of these sacred Sounds is "Om." It contains the principles of centripetal and centrifugal forces, namely: "If the Sound dies, the earth will die." This sacred Sound is so important that numerous rules, which have literally become tabu, have fixed its use, pronunciation, and intonation. The primordial elements earth, water, light, air, and ether were grouped together at the time the words were formed through the power of the bija-mantra. When I say "taru," a Sanskrit word meaning "tree," there is a word-form connected with a creative mantra just as the pulsation in my veins is the vibration of Shakti.

Without a strict initiation and all the conditions required of purification on all levels, the bija-mantra is never revealed to the seeker. Few are the disciples who pass through the narrow gate, but many others have their lives completely filled only by one single fleeting vision of Shakti, or of its intellectual knowledge, or its invocation. Two powers are necessary for these latter disciples: "A constant and infallible aspiration calling from below and a supreme Grace responding from above."* And further: "The gift of self must be total and extend to all parts of the being." It is only in these conditions that Shakti can manifest itself.

Shakti is the mystery of mysteries. One should think about it in this way. It is the unique center, the Void of all religions. All the incarnations, prophets, initiates, and enlightened ones have drunk from this source and drink there constantly. They have known or they know oneness, and they share with us what they are able to express of their bliss. Their accounts and their teachings are almost identical even though their disciples, after having analyzed the sensations resulting from their own experience, give mental explanations that become dogmas.

Among all the countries of the world, what is par-

*Shri Aurobindo, *The Mother* (Adyar).

ticular to India is that, in Hinduism, Shakti is not confined exclusively to temples or to sacred places to the
extent that it is in other religions. Just as the Ganges
overflows its banks as it flows from the Himalayas to
the sea, Shakti overflows the esotericism of the temples, allowing itself to be caught in the eyes of the
God-mad* beggars whom one meets everywhere. The
overflow of spiritual force, in the midst of luxuriant
and tropical nature, explains the need for restrictive
laws of castes governing the orthodox Hindu society,
namely the ninety-five percent of the total population.
These laws are based far more on the need to create
a line of demarcation that protects Shakti than on
economic considerations, which were thought of much
later.

The fixation of the Divine Shakti, by the priest who
pronounces a mantra, into the principle of oneness,
"spirit-matter,"is really the heart of the puja,†which
signifies bringing life into an image. Shakti is im-
mobilized and becomes then a bridge between the bija-

*Saintly wanderers known as bauls, they are poets and
singers, belong to no caste, and have no dogma or rites.
†The ceremony of adoration performed every day.

mantra and the image. When all the required conditions are fulfilled, the life transmitted produces a transformation of substance which is as total and absolute as in the mystery of the Eucharist. When the adoration is ended, with its offerings and sacrifices, the priest pronounces another mantra, which frees what was bound and liberates Shakti from the image of wood or stone, the bowl of water, or the fire which was momentarily its receptacle. During the puja, every particle of the image becomes the real Divine Presence. For this reason the officiating priest, after having established the limit of the sacred Sound of Shakti with a red thread, says, invoking Shakti: "Until the puja is terminated, grant us the grace to dwell in this form." If Shakti were not liberated at the end of the puja, the Divine Substance would remain as alive as a consecrated Host in a ciborium. Such cases are known. India also has certain temples where Shakti has been permanently fixed in an image. From this flows a constant ritual as if a puja was being celebrated without end.

Among Christians, some believe and others do not believe in the real Presence of Christ in the Sacred Host.

The Hindus are also divided. There are those who see in Shakti the oneness of spirit-matter, and they are legion, and there are those who believe that spirit and matter are like water and oil, well mixed but without losing their true nature. Between these two conceptions, both groups reveal the secret of the point of contact between them. That contact is in "that which is limitless" in the moving and living density of these two propositions: Shakti, or spirit, is tenuous and subtle; and Shiva, or matter, is heavy and dense. Everything is a play of converging densities. Matter can be so tenuous that it becomes invisible and spirit can be so dense that it becomes perceptible. Such is the movement in Shakti, which man cannot grasp, much less discuss.

It is perfectly childish, illogical, and false to accuse the Hindu of pantheism when one sees him offering to the Divine Shakti as a receptacle a black pebble, a bowl of water, fire, a flower, and a thousand other things, not to mention images of stone or wood. All these varied forms have no more value than the un-leavened bread of the Christians. The receptacle means little—only the life of the real Presence, the Divine Power, has meaning.

After the celebration of the puja, the Hindu throws
into the Ganges the image in which Shakti has dwelt,*
so as to sever any attachment that he might have de-
veloped with it. He remains open to other manifesta-
tions of Shakti as he is always eager to seek liberated
ones who could help him. To come into the presence
of a liberated one is to taste the bliss of a saint and
to give birth spontaneously to the desire to live at his
feet and to absorb something of Shakti. Thus, the disciple becomes for a long time like mistletoe on a tree,
living in the grace of his master and supported by it.
His effort often stops there or he becomes a valuable
instrument and uses Shakti for useful work in the
world. Other disciples, after having drunk from the
cup of Shakti, are intoxicated forever. Because they
have tasted the divine nectar, they, like madmen
searching for the needle in a haystack, only desire
solitude and a "life in the forest." Nature is a powerful
aid for entering into the play of the Divine Shakti.
Because of its impersonal character, the duality of
good and evil is harmonized in it more quickly than
in the world. Its silence stills the mind, which always

* At the time of great celebrations like the Durga puja, in Bengal.

tries to explain Shakti instead of feeling it. At this moment it can be said that the seekers are carried away by the force of Shakti. They remount the current toward the source of pure enjoyment of Shakti. Strange journey! Shakti then manifests itself with equal force in the eye of a saint, in the perfume of a flower, the blue of the sky, or the sacred Sound. Forms vanish because they become transparent as crystal; the inner and outer are no longer separated except by light.

From this moment, one single thing counts—"That" in the breath and in the blood. A puja becomes as refreshing as a bowl of milk at the side of the road, a mountain stream, or the smile of a child. Everything is a help, nothing more, everything is temporary, fleeting, out of time. One thing only remains: the relation of cause to effect in Shakti.

Meditation is really a repose in Shakti. It is a state similar to that of a heart that would cease to beat in order to feel the joy of the rebirth of life. To meditate in Shakti is to abandon all forms, all dogmas, and all gurus. But this knowledge settles in oneself slowly, only after a very long period of submission in which guru, dogmas, and forms are indispensable. First of all it is necessary to be firmly anchored in devotion to an Ishta* in order to make the slightest progress. The effort demanded is illustrated by the following story:

A master had his disciple meditate on a buffalo in a cell next to him. After six months of meditation the guru called his disciple, who quickly got up to answer him. Six months later the disciple did the same again and the master sent him back to his meditation; but a year later, when the master called, the disciple began to weep: "Oh master, I would very much like to come, but the door is too narrow, my horns will never get through!"

It is from the moment when concentration on the form is perfected that the liquefaction of the form can begin. Shakti is then at work in both senses. The path of meditation in Shakti is as narrow as the razor's edge because Shakti works to unlink spirit and matter as it had originally linked them to be fully adored and served. One must be thoroughly prepared and supported to confront this stage in which the least opposition of the disciple to the divine vibration would lead to the depths of disturbance. It is necessary to go for-

* The adored form of the Divine.

ward on this path with complete humility and not play with the Divine Force before it makes itself manifest.

It is said that a disciple wanted, after a long austerity, to live off this Force. The master, to whom he addressed himself, said, "If you think yourself ready, enter into this cave. Meditate unceasingly with eyes closed. Refuse every vision except that of your Ishta. Once each day leave your cave. Near the opening flows a spring beside a fruit tree. Drink one mouthful of water, pluck a single fruit, and return to your meditation." The disciple followed these orders to the letter, but on the ninth day after having eaten the fruit, he was suddenly tempted to pluck a second one. When he bit into this fruit the earth trembled. The cave disappeared with the tree and the spring, and he found himself hurled to the ground, dying of a hunger such as he had never felt!

Such is the lesson of Shakti, when, reason obscuring intuition, the vision of the seeker is momentarily disturbed. But the moment of grace exists; it is in the very fact that Shakti joins all things together. This immutable link between the creature and his Creator is the very grace of Shakti.

Part Two

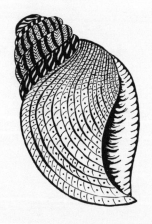

This great Divine Force of Shakti moves in the silence. But not in the silence as defined by a dictionary: "State of a person who abstains from talking, omission of an explanation, absence of noise, whence a second definition: peace and inaction in a figurative sense." Here we have a complete negation of everything connected to the realm of thought, soul, and vital movement. India knows a silence that is positive even though it has the same negative appearance. This silence explains all problems, since thought returns to its seed. Figuratively speaking, it is the most encompassing action one might conceive in the struggle between the secret tendencies of the individual. It is the silence of which one becomes aware beyond all doubt; as for example, when seated at the feet of Ramana Maharshi.

But there is yet another silence that contains in itself the positive silence and the negative silence, and that is the very one in which Shakti moves. It is in this silence that the great masters, or the liberated ones, dwell, no matter to what religion they belong. The way in which their story is told has little importance. A cloud, flames, waves, or even a halo is often used to represent the realm of indefinable mystery that separates the ordinary man from the liberated one; namely, the ordinary man, who lives in dualities, as compared to the liberated one, who lives beyond dualities. In fact there is something akin to fear in the obeisance of one who prostrates himself, or in the hard and rigid attitude of one who reasons before that which eludes him. The fact is that a zone of opaque silence separates man from saint and, still more, man from God. In man the same zone of silence also separates his ego from his soul, and this is why there are so many secret struggles, tears, and so much anguish among lovers and those who are solitary and dissatisfied.

This silence of Shakti is a void, full and whole, a perfect harmony. When silence radiates from the center of Shakti and allows itself to be seen, it is the fullness of contemplation. When silence is a moment of grace between God and man, it becomes the sudden joy of the one who meditates.

On the path of meditation, one follows the precise instructions of the guru because one has asked for them, and because one feels the ground slipping at each step. This insecurity is one of the characteristics of silence, which one senses and which extends between the deed and its consequences, between real life and the life of dreams. It is in this silence that one sees the smile of the Ishta, who little by little loses his human traits as he passes toward the center of Shakti. This is a general rule. Numerous examples can be given. Krishna is described as being a complete incarnation; Buddha and Jesus are now hardly ever referred to as men; Shri Ramakrishna and Shri Sarada Devi are considered to be in the process of passing through the narrow gate. The great liberated ones of India, such as Shri Aurobindo, Ramana Maharshi, Ma Ananda Moyi—and there are still others—whose teachings are now known in the West, have the power of Shakti in their look. It is in silence that they are the Absolute. To succeed in creating an eternal image of divine beings there will for many years be need of veneration and fidelity in their disciples in order to destroy the human elements that tie them still to the earth, and to tradition. Blessed be these disciples, who forge for generations to come a scale of values absolutely necessary for faith and reason, for the purpose of attaining the silence of Shakti.

If the master is still alive, he is quite apart from the

efforts that his disciples are making. For him his time of trial is accomplished; he has passed through the hellfire of great personal discipline before being worshipped. He is at the same time flesh and a mystical symbol. He is the haven of beatitude and pure abstraction of "That" so perfectly harmonized in Shakti. Blessed be the cloud which veils the radiant knowledge of Shakti, since we are not yet ready! It allows us to invoke: "My guru, Thou art Shiva, the Great Lord, Thou art the instrument of destruction and creation, that which is born in death. I am Thou, and me in Thou."

On the path of meditation there are pauses of rest that are precisely this silence of grace. This silence has dual qualities. It is the moment in which the rising wave of aspiration toward God meets the descending wave. It is also the moment often broken by the fear of the disciple, provoked by the positive and negative aspects playing together in the silence believed to be static. Later, without the quality of silence having changed, anguish rises when silence ceases. After the silence there is the unknown, in which one dares not venture. To let go what one holds without knowing what will happen is heroism! Then each return into life after having tasted this silence calls for an adjustment. All the saints who climb upward toward Tibet, to the abode of Shiva on Mount Kailas, have described in detail their pilgrimage. They go on living from one renunciation through another. On this arduous path creative silence is constantly renewed.

This silence is the result of a difficult and prolonged concentration that easily becomes irritating. This concentration is the very discipline which enables the camel to pass through the eye of a needle. And it is not easy. Stubborn obedience in spite of a thousand temptations, a sense of loyalty, and a desire for purification illuminate the period of self-denial. "The hand of my guru has marked my forehead with the sacred ashes, the ashes of my own life." But this silvered ash is not death. One must find this for oneself through the grace of revelation. The death that the ash symbolizes is truly the birth in an element more subtle than matter.

The silence of Shakti dwells in the Himalayas. Tradition affirms it. Sadhus and hermits live there in voluntary solitude to absorb it. Their life remains a mystery woven with the supernatural. The attraction of this silence is so powerful that many are the people from the plains who live in the hope of making a pilgrimage there. There are temples in the mountains where the veil of Shakti is torn, giving a fleeting vision that fills one's whole life with beatitude.

This silence exerts an undeniable attraction by the very contradiction that goes with it. All the sages affirm that there is a completeness in this silence, whereas life leaves a bitter aftertaste. And as it is said: "An empty cup will satisfy you more than a full one." From this comes the desire to escape from the waves of past impressions to go toward this silence which is completeness. One wishes to leave the plains, with the refinements of an easy life, and go toward the simple life of a mountain people, where art is nature and love is the earth and sky. Each man who rules his family with a heavy hand loves to imagine himself meditating on the ashes of renunciation. He lives one role and speaks of another just as the sadhu living in austerity will for a long time think of what he left behind. These contrasts mark the long path with resting places of realization.

For him who is on the path, these moments of realization are grace, as each disciple believes his guru to be the Absolute. Through these partial realizations one must affirm one's vision according to a scale of values that one can trust. It is in this security that a new understanding is built in which the being will seek its own expansion. Powers come and go, affirmations and negations rise up and die in the abyss of silence. After a lifetime of work one aspires to this confrontation with oneself. It is to love death as one loves life; it is to enter into and to be in Shakti, both at the same time. One often hears the saying: "In the Himalayas it is not necessary to believe in anything at all. Though you be an agnostic or a rebel, the sanctified earth prays in your stead and leads you to the goal!" The mountains are alive. They continue to rise more than a centimeter each year toward the sky, sometimes violently shaking their masses of granite and shale. Certain pilgrims go there to attain a precise aim in spiritual realization within a fixed time—such are the landowners who amass property and gold until they are fifty years old, then stop and give themselves to God with the same intensity with which they had become rich. Shri Sarada

Devi, with her practical sense, said one day to one of her disciples, "Do you believe, my son, that God can be bought like a fish in the marketplace?"

He who enters into the silence of Shakti is like a mustard seed between millstones that crush it to make oil. A slow process of purification is necessary, which is more or less conscious. The disciple lives in his thoughts, body, and movements in the obedience which he has accepted of his guru. He takes refuge in his personal discipline or in the orthodoxy of the laws of his caste, whose rights and limitations are well known to him. If there is no spiritual group to support him, he creates one for himself through self-imposed laws. The forms prescribed by Shakti are innumerable. The itinerant monk, who is the prototype of an anti-social being, has a discipline no less strict. This submission is imperative and necessary in order to taste the supreme freedom of the soul. Even Christians, attracted by one or another form of Hinduism, become even more orthodox than the most austere Brahmins. This is clearly one of the rules of spiritual life. Rare are the liberated ones who search for nothing more, who live simply and joyously the "what is" in the present moment. This is why the mountains echo with so many calls: "Hara, Hara!" or "Hari, Hari!" or "Ram, Ram!" everyone seeing the Universal in these. The wind brings all voices into one, the mountains sparkle, distant and cold. The old earth also advises: "Do not speak of your spiritual experience, so slippery is the path."

A very, very long pilgrimage in silence is necessary, until little by little values diminish and blend. All mountains bear the name of a seer and are crowned by a temple dedicated to a goddess. The mountains have one voice, that of the wind, whose sound "Om" strikes their steep sides, starts avalanches, and carries away the earth. The Divine Force comes down from the summits while men from the lands below strive to conquer the heights of the gods, where realization exists in ultimate silence! The town of Almora is proud of its recent electrification and is now talking about irrigation. Is free India now going to establish Alpine stations such as the Swiss have, and drive away the gods from their abodes? The great Himalayan expanse is the unknown zone where dwells the silence of Shakti. Man needs to have this refuge, to know where the gods live until he knows that his real self and his soul are one.

The silence of Shakti, source of creation, like the ecstasy of the saints, is inexplicable. The first element to die is speech, because there is nothing more to be said. This is not a retreat. But the lips are silent because forms and densities have become one and the same force. All efforts and all paths disappear. A single ladder of light leans against the wall of the garden of knowledge. And the pilgrim climbs the ladder. At the top, he skins his hands and arms to scale the last rocks. He does not look back. He leaps into the garden of knowledge.

In the silence of Shakti thought melts. Shakti dismantles and dissolves it. Thought is no longer "that which one sets before oneself to meditate and then to take up again." Thought is now separate, but is still in the air one breathes, in the water one drinks, in the flower one smells. It is in the vibration of Shakti.

In a small refuge, an itinerant monk is seated, legs crossed. He has no name. His face is as calm as a mask of death, his eyes are gazing into the unknown.

*31*

"What exists in the silence of Shakti when all movement stops?"

"There is the Void to allow you to find again your starting point."

"But I no longer see this starting point. Where is it?"

"Find it in your own vibration."

"But I only wish to go forward."

"If you follow the forward movement, once the circle is closed you will become the inner space. You cannot be this inner space without closing the circle."

This monk had lived for twelve years in a silence seldom interrupted. On the ground a coarse handwoven rug, whitewashed walls, the door open to the plains, terrace after terrace.

I placed in front of the monk a napkin filled with fruit. In the silence there was not the least thought, the least vibration. The look from one to the other was a mirror of eternity. Then the monk said, "Enter into me, and know."

Such is the silence of Shakti.

# Part Three

One of the most important vows in spiritual life is the vow of silence. Everyone knows that Gandhi did not speak on Mondays. All the explanations that are given for this are correct. And furthermore, Monday is the special day consecrated to the Divine Power, to the active Shakti. Shakti is also the Divine Mother, whose name is repeated in prayer with an insistent wish for purification. On this day many women fast in order to be a living link between the Divine Mother and their families and to obtain special grace for those they love.

There are several degrees in the spiritual discipline of silence. It is an exercise of control which many gurus impose on themselves and which they also advise or command their disciples to do, according to their needs. This exercise provides a solid mental support. This silence—silence of thought and silence of speech— is but a crutch necessary while a new understanding builds in one who is searching for the light.

Many monks in India live in the silence of Shakti. The signs that appear to be negative—not to speak, not to see, not to hear, not to taste or smell—are only the stages of a transformation in which intelligence

*36*

dissociates itself from the various senses. There are still other more subtle disciplines that escape all external observation. What the ascetic experiences at the height of his effort or what the disciple knows at the feet of his guru can only be explained by closed lips. When they speak, it is in short aphorisms. In their presence, one must bow, remembering this: "He who speaks knows nothing. He who knows is mute." Closed lips are the door of Shakti.

The closed lips of "he who knows" are gentle and smiling. They make you think of flowers. "Have you ever seen a flower cry?" At first the lips open and say, "A mountain is a mountain and a waterfall is a waterfall." Then comes a long period when the lips remain silent. It is a time of inner work, when a mountain is no longer a mountain, when a waterfall is no longer a waterfall. It is also a period of effort, during which the lips contain the breath, control, swallow, or exhale it. It is also the period when the lips choose only pure nourishment, repeat prayers, sometimes trembling from doubt and tensed by fear, until the day when all the values change. Thus the mountain is once again a mountain and the waterfall is once again a waterfall.

But there are no words to express it. It is direct experience. The smile alone reveals the living secret of Shakti.

The door of Shakti is not more tightly closed than are the living lips, for Shakti is life itself. All the potential for higher development is guarded behind this door. This is why those who sit at the feet of a guru experience something of the anguish of the young bride of Bluebeard when she held in her hand the key to the forbidden door. Most disciples remain prudently at a respectful distance. They wish very much to know what is inside the door of Shakti while remaining outside! They have many excuses: "I am in the presence of a being who attained liberation through long asceticism or an incarnation of the Divine Spirit born through its own power. The being before me dwells in Shakti, moves in Shakti. He is no longer touched by the waves of impressions in which I live." In conclusion, fewer are the human elements and more apparent the divine elements, but the distance is greater.

The closed lips of a saint only give what can be absorbed. Therein lies the security of the disciple. Each one has a feeling of fullness, which becomes his understanding of the Absolute. It is a positive, personal assurance that one gives oneself to counterbalance the fear of the Void, which is so keenly felt. The disciple seeks himself in the reflection of him who knows all things. This silence of the guru, as the quest of the disciple, are one and the same in the silence of Shakti.

When Ma Ananda Moyi was asked, "Are you the Divine Mother?" she replied: "I am what you see in me." To the same question Shri Sarada Devi replied: "I hold the manifestation of God in my hand." Another guru responded vaguely: "I am the fire, I am the wind, I am the sun." The veil before closed lips is transparent for some disciples. Some others see the veil as a wall and run into it like sheep. No flame can burn it, no weapon can tear it. All action dies in the Void.

The vibration of Shakti is so strong that it would cause an explosion if it were confined. Just as the lips are slightly open from inner pressure, so a temple has its door or gates partly opened with a guard at its entrance. In certain temples these guards are terrifying gods of stone or watchdogs with bulging eyes. The vibration of Shakti that dwells in the sacred image of the temple has the same force as that in the seed awaiting the right time to germinate. A grain of wheat or rice is still alive after thousands of years. The patience of Shakti is infinite because it has neither a beginning nor end; it constantly renews itself in its two movements: that which goes toward the exterior, creating new forms without ceasing, and that which goes toward the interior, inhaling all life and leading it back to its source.

The vibration of Shakti becomes the mystery of creation the moment it manifests itself out of the Void. This passage of the Divine Shakti is often represented as an exhalation through a mask without jaws—an ancient and crude symbol—which expresses how that which is inside is forced outside. It is at this moment that the breath condenses into vapor, fluids, and forms that are at first vague. Then the subtle densities gradually become heavier until they are matter. It is life at its birth, with all its aspects of duality on its way to complete its course of involution. This purpose accomplished, it has another course of evolution to complete in order to return to its starting point. It is here that God and nature, man and his soul, are one, with a flow of life including both paradise and hell, and the soul keeping watch with a vague awareness of the original light.

The road is long until the individual soul becomes conscious enough to stop the movement that takes it away. From this moment, without will, word, or thought, it rediscovers within itself the vibration of Shakti. It is the "Kingdom of Heaven" within oneself, the beatitude, and the divine smile of all eternity. The veils that obscured the light fall away. "Who are you?" asks Shri Sarada Devi of Kali the Divine Mother, who appears unexpectedly. "I am your sister," replies the Divine Shakti with a very sweet voice. "Fear nothing, the same blood flows in our veins, the same warmth. All is so simple. Ask nothing. Look into my eyes, we are one soul."

All the great spiritual beings have entered the Void, the inner circle of Shakti. That which in them remains a mystery for us is the ultimate unknown which they reflect. It is their secret. Their desire to reveal their experience to us stops at the very moment when we can no longer absorb what they have to transmit. We alone are at fault. It is for us to become worthy of the light that comes to meet us. What we wish to ignore as long as possible is that their sacrifice stands between them and us. This sacrifice is to remain on our level, to be with us. We do not have the courage to face it even though we wish to derive all possible benefits from it. This sacrifice is expiation in many forms and under many different names. It is the vanishing of dualities on all levels, the oneness of Purusha-Prakriti. It is the One beyond spirit and matter.

What is infinitely touching is the "temporary attachment," often childish, that most of the great gurus agree upon to remain in communication with us, heart to heart. What kindness! for it cannot be denied that the guru frightens us a little by his impartiality and objectivity. This is so true that Semitic religions have turned him into the "Judge." Shakti is "what is." If it is dual, it is the day and the night. If it is beyond what is dual, it is the Absolute.

The stillness of this Absolute is creative silence. Therein a "new movement" is being born, the essence of life. Shakti seeks to manifest itself like a child at birth. Certain of the liberated ones have spent several years in the creative silence of Shakti before opening their lips. All have known the desert and its temptations, for it is a work of creation which can be neither forced nor hurried. It no longer belongs to the consciousness of the I. That is why the lips remain closed. It is the beginning and the end of creation, which has neither beginning nor end.

Part Four

Between God and his worshipper there is a pathway of light, visible or invisible. This pathway is Shakti. The rainbow, which our eyes needed to see after the flood, in order to be assured of the alliance with God, is clearly an outward sign of divine grace. There are other pathways of light that are invisible and that faith alone perceives. No believer doubts this. Artists, poets, dreamers, scientists know it. One rarely speaks of it.

When Shakti functions as a balance between two points, it is static, immobile, and unconscious in its dormant power. It unites opposites. It is their essence and their relationship as well as their support. In spiritual life this third element of Shakti as a balance is seldom mentioned. However, the following image is given: Shakti, personified by the goddess Parvati, is leaning against Shiva, who looks far into the distance, into the Void. The force of Shakti is asleep. As soon as Shiva lowers his eyes and looks at Parvati, a question arises: "Am I Thou? Art Thou me?" As soon as this dual consciousness is awakened, worlds are created and forms spring forth. The static balance continues to exist to harmonize the work of Shakti in its infinite capacity of creating forms.

It is thus that Shakti becomes the pathway between the disciple and his guru, while for the disciple the guru becomes the aim in itself. The guru and the disciple represent the necessary opposites who call to each other, fulfill each other, complete each other. They only exist, one through the other, within their respective functions. To speak of the pathway between them would be absurd; they are a unity with two distinct aspects. The equilibrium between them is the moment they meet in the Absolute.

Both guru and disciple, if they are pure in their intentions, make their way toward the Absolute. This point of meeting in the Absolute is described in all the scriptures. The Buddhists call it "satori"; the Christians, "the mystical union"; in India, it is often described as the moment of realization, when the disciple sinks into the light, crying, *"Soham . . . Soham!* I am He . . . I am He!" The guru has vanished. In reality the disciple has always been the guru and the guru the disciple. As opposites they are the same thing manifested in different densities. To reach this point of realization, it must be understood that, because of the law of attraction, the law of "self-defense" is in full force at each of the two poles. Even the liberated ones cannot escape it. They have their duties, and there is a continual rhythm of movement inward and outward all around them. Certain disciples who have touched realization choose to remain the rest of their lives at the feet of the guru in order to savor the love that unites them. Certain gurus give of themselves endlessly in an impersonal way. The guru and the disciple are like an old married couple between whom a static equilibrium has become their support.

The circle of the power of Shakti is so complete that it is as difficult to get out of it as it is to get into it. The meeting of the guru and the disciple is the same as "love at first sight" between two lovers. There is no logic or human law to prevent such meeting of souls. A force draws them together in spite of themselves. They are carried along by their destiny. Families are sometimes broken: husbands, wives, and children abandoned. Tears are the opposite of happiness before the contrasts are erased in the equilibrium of Shakti. For the disciple, the guru becomes the great womb of creation that envelops everything, shapes everything, giving life and devouring it with inexpressible tenderness and harshness. All this is preparing for the moment when all is revealed.

Getting out of the circle of power is no less difficult. When the power has been transmitted from the guru to the disciple who is consciously or unconsciously ready, inevitably there is a separation—a poignant moment with a cruel question. Two tigers cannot live in the same forest. The guru drives the disciple out or the disciple leaves. In this separation the relationship that exists between a seed and the mother-plant remains. That is all. A new vibration is born in freedom.

To speak of the moment of realization is the secret ambition of each disciple. One longs to have a companion with whom to talk about one's aim. One likes to describe each effort, each difficulty. The disciples are on the lookout for every change in their inner attitude. But in reality one never speaks of the contact with the Absolute, which alone matters. One speaks in detail of the ecstasy of others, reading and analyzing descriptions of them. Sometimes one ascribes to oneself the experiences of very advanced disciples and as a consequence the soul is tortured with unfulfilled desires.

When the vibrations of Shakti are very close to us, we avoid speaking of the moment of going to sleep and of the moment of awakening. Why is this? At that point, the equilibrium of Shakti resembles the approach of death. We like to forget it. One vaguely remembers having been taught to pray at this very moment. It is not the words that matter but the attitude of submission necessary to capture the rhythm of a different and greater consciousness. We go to sleep, without fear, confident that in the morning our body will be awakened with its well-regulated animal life. But if this sleep were to be death? We do not know what the life of the soul is when awakened on the other side of the veil! We fear because we have forgotten that the path of invisible light is within us, the beginning and the end of life.

In India, the concept of Shakti, being an element of equilibrium, gives to the whole life a quality that is quite remarkable. It attenuates all forms and blurs what we call a "fact." This is why life is less clear-cut than in the West and is constantly mixed with daydreams and different values of time and space. In an abstract sense of Shakti, life gives to man an extrahuman dimension, which has nothing to do with the concept of paradise or hell. It is rather a sense of continuity of power, which passes from one generation to another without any logic. Thus very pious men or women sometimes see their own spiritual realization being lived, not by themselves, but by one of their grandchildren born with the benefit of all their accumulated merits, and with the true intuition of those who know all things.

How can Shakti dwell in a small child? I know a little girl who has a smile of perfection on her lips and the look of the Infinite in her eyes. With no effort, with no thought, she is just a very small girl!

"Why am I moved to cry when I look at this child?"

"Because you see the Infinite in her eyes."

"And why do I tremble?"

"Because the Soul of God is being reflected in you . . ."

When I asked the child, "Who are you?" she answered with a smile, surprising her parents: "I am Atman."* And she began to play with the flowers I had given to her. She is just three years old. She knows nothing of the world and has not yet been taught anything. But she is in herself the Divine Mother born out of ultimate wisdom. She is a living experience. She knows things in the realm of the soul in the same way

* The universal divine soul.

as child prodigies hear uncreated music that carries them on the wings of a dream. This little girl has in her the purity of the virgins who, through the ages, have borne the Son of the Spirit each time He has appeared among men "because it was necessary." She is also the reflection of light for those in need of love. In her, time stands still. Shakti manifests itself so openly that one does not know how to honor it and at the same time protect the child—for she is just a little girl.

Thus the great Shakti takes sometimes unexpected forms. The Divine Power incarnates itself unceasingly, it is capricious and deaf, but it hears the footsteps of ants. Its worshippers without ceasing beg it to manifest itself. Men think much and want many things, and in so doing create the chaos in which we search for our path. Nature does not think: it is a great vessel of power that is offered to invigorate us. The seers of Vedic times knew of this marriage of heaven and earth; they lived in the vibration of Shakti. "Thou art man, Thou art woman, Thou art the adolescent going forward and the young girl adorned. Thou are also the old man tottering on his crutches."

Many are the forms that Shakti assumes.

*A Note About the Author*

Lizelle Reymond spent ten years of her life
in the Himalayas, mostly in Almora, studying and
working with Shri Anirvan. The two books describing
her life and the teaching she received there have now
been translated and published in the United States.
They are *My Life with a Brahmin Family*
and *To Live Within*.
Between 1935 and 1953, she translated several
sacred texts on Indian wisdom and these were
published in France.
Now Lizelle Reymond lives in Geneva; she is
at work on her third book, which will contain
many letters from Shri Anirvan.

*A Note on the Type*

The text of this book was set in a film version
of Palatino, a type face designed by the noted
German typographer Hermann Zapf.
Named after Giovambattista Palatino,
a writing master of Renaissance Italy,
Palatino was the first of Zapf's type faces
to be introduced to America. The first designs
for the face were made in 1948, and the fonts for the
complete face were issued between 1950 and 1952.
Like all Zapf-designed type faces, Palatino
is beautifully balanced and exceedingly readable.

Composed by University Graphics, Inc.,
Shrewsbury, New Jersey.
Printed and bound by The Book Press, Inc.,
Brattleboro, Vermont.

Tantric drawings by Madhur Jaffrey.
Design by Betty Anderson.